God Forgives Sinners

by
W.E.Best

SOUTH BELT GRACE CHURCH
10603 BLACKHAWK BLVD.
P.O. BOX 34904
HOUSTON, TEXAS 77234-4904

God Forgives Sinners

Contents

Introduction

Sinners are at enmity with God, whose name is "holy and reverend" (Ps. 111:9). As omnipotence is the power of God's attributes, holiness is their beauty. Holiness is self-affirming purity. God's omnipotence declares Him mighty, and His holiness declares Him glorious. Just as the sun's loss of light would cause it to lose its heat and quickening virtue, God's loss of holiness would cause Him to lose His quickening power. Sinners want God to satisfy their lusts on earth; they would dethrone God and degrade His character. God, however surrenders to no one.

Holiness is God's chief attribute, and it can never be attained by any man. (Who can equal God?) God's love is important, but that is not His fundamental attribute. Love requires a standard, and its standard is holiness. God's love is regulated not by sentiment but by principle. Grace reigns not at the expense of righteousness but *through* righteousness (Rom. 5:21). God's love never conflicts with His holiness.

God is the God of order. There is order in the Godhead, in salvation, and in service. Order in the Godhead is God the Father, God the Son, and God the Holy Spirit. That order does not imply, however, that the character of the Father is greater than that of either the

9

Son or the Holy Spirit. Order in the Godhead is revealed in authority. The Father so loved His own elect among sinners that He sent His Son into the world—Jesus Christ came. The Lord Jesus Christ ascended after His death and resurrection and sent the Holy Spirit—the Holy Spirit came. The One sent was not less in character but in authority. The Father planned salvation for the elect in eternity past; the Son purchased the elect's salvation two thousand years ago when He died on the cross; the Holy Spirit applies the salvation that the Father planned and the Son purchased to the hearts of the elect in time.

There is also order in the application of salvation to the elect: first comes regeneration, then conversion. Regeneration, which comes from God alone, occurs when the Holy Spirit enters the heart of an individual sinner and gives him a desire for spiritual things. Regeneration is identical in every individual; conversion experiences, however, vary.

There is order also in the true conversion experience of a man who has been regenerated. His mind, emotions, and will are affected. His regeneration by the Spirit of God gives him a disposition for the things of God. When such a person hears the gospel proclaimed, his mind is set in motion. He hears and understands. In this way the intellectual part of man is engaged in a true conversion experience. His God-imparted, inward disposition enables him to recognize truth when he hears it (John 10:4-5), and he responds to that truth.

Sinners—enemies of God—offend the Lord. They manifest irreverence for Him and reject His Son and His Word. They seek preeminence for themselves, instead of recognizing God's preeminence. Therefore, they have no hope apart from God's everlasting forgiveness through grace.

Everlastingly forgiven persons still need restorative forgiveness. Although sinners are forgiven through justification, saints are forgiven through sanctification. Jesus Christ, the saints' Advocate, keeps them safe, and their

10

confession of sins keeps them in fellowship. Because every Christian sins, every Christian requires continual sanctification. That is why the Lord Jesus Christ intercedes for the saints at the right hand of the Father.

God's character, which is light, reveals the sins of saints to themselves. But failure to confess these sins causes Christians to lose fellowship with the Lord. Children of light who walk in darkness cannot fellowship with God who is Light. On the other hand, instruction, blessing, and service follow confession; revived believers produce fruit.

Although Christians are restored from backsliding after confession, God does chastise them for their sins (see Gal. 6:7). Divine principles do not change, and the failure of Christians to conform to these principles brings God's chastening hand upon His children.

The subject of forgiveness cannot be properly approached apart from the biblical concept of sin, its origins, and its consequences. Therefore, before we begin the discussion of forgiveness, let us briefly summarize the beginning and result of sin. A person cannot fully appreciate forgiveness unless he knows who has forgiven him and of what he has been forgiven.

1

Sin Decreed by
the Forgiver

——————— DEUTERONOMY 29:29 ———————

God does not have two wills: "But he is in one mind, and who can turn him? and what his soul desireth, even that he doeth" (Job 23:13). There is in that one will a *revealed* and a *concealed* hemisphere: "The secret things belong unto the Lord our God: but those things which are revealed belong unto us and to our children for ever, that we may do all the words of this law" (Deut. 29:29). God has seen fit not to reveal His complete will to men. He reveals only what is needed by men while they are pilgrims on the earth.

God keeps many things partially secret, but He has no intention of keeping them secret forever. When Christians stand before the Lord, they shall learn more about the mysteries associated with the Godhead. They will understand predestination, imputation, and every biblical doctrine. Throughout the ceaseless ages of eternity, the Lord will continue to reveal to His own the exceeding riches of His grace.

The will of God can be compared to a sphere. One can see only part of a sphere at a time. We can see only one side of the moon; the same is true with the sun and the earth. The whole sphere of a planet cannot be seen at one time. Truth is like a sphere. No one sees or knows all truth. Men are responsible to know and obey the revealed part of truth, but they are not responsible for that which is concealed.

God is omniscient; His understanding is infinite: "Great is our Lord, and of great power: his understanding is infinite" (Ps. 147:5). God's will or purpose or decree is *one sphere.*

God's decree to permit sin was included in the secret part of His will. But man's sin was, in a sense, necessary to God's purpose in Christ. God did allow sin, but that does not designate Him the author of sin. One cannot believe that God is sovereign without also believing that He allowed sin. If God had not allowed Adam's fall, it could not have occurred. He also purposed that Jesus Christ should come and die for sin—the Son of God is the Lamb that was slain from the foundation of the world (Rev. 13:8). Jesus Christ died for the sins of the elect according to the purpose of God.

God created Adam upright. Adam had no sin within, but he was capable of sinning; that is, his uprightness was finite. Sin began among mankind after Adam's creation.

The apparent inconsistency of God decreeing sin, yet not being the author of sin, is explained when one realizes that God's *purpose* is not the *originating cause* of man's sin. These things are inexplicable to an unsaved person. He can, however, recognize that sin exists. And when he recognizes sin's actuality, he will also recognize that he is guilty of sin.

Since God created man in His own image and after His likeness, sin could not have been part of Adam's nature. If sin had been a part, we would have to conclude that either Adam was a being that did not have God as his author, or that God is the author of sin.

Sin exists, but no one can explain its origin. We do know, however, that since sin came into the world it has become the motive for all thoughts and actions of men.

The Bible describes man's sin as *personal*—each individual is the cause of his own sin. Throughout the Scriptures, sin is represented as one's own. Men are admonished not to make any neutral or objective investigation of sin's origin (Gen. 3), because no person will confess sin so long as he seeks to know its origin. There is no excuse: "... their own doings have beset them about ..." (Hos. 7:2). Sin is personal, and blame for it cannot be shifted to parents, environment, or anything but oneself. Sin proceeds from *within* individual hearts (Mark 7:21-23).

Reconciliation is the act of God: "God was in Christ, reconciling the world unto himself, not imputing their trespasses unto them; and hath committed unto us the word of reconciliation" (II Cor. 5:19). The necessity for reconciliation attests man's guilt before God. Jesus Christ became the Surety for the elect; the elect become reconciled to God through His Son and God in His grace forgives them for their sins.

The Lord controls every move and heartbeat on earth ("For in him we live, and move, and have our being," Acts 17:28), and He allows man to commit sin. However, He does not cooperate in the evil committed by any person; He only allows it. All things work according to God's plan; providence is God's plan in execution. The Lord is working out His own purpose in time for the Christian's good and His own glory.

The fact that all things work according to God's pleasure is frequently misunderstood. We see many who appear to be masters of their own conduct, acting by their knowledge and choice and possessing boundless liberty and capricious dispositions. They are governed sometimes by principle, sometimes by example, sometimes by pride, and sometimes by peer pressure. Since men are unable to distinguish the first cause from the subordinate issue, the chief agent from the instrument, the Creator's perfection from the creature's weakness, they attribute man's action to himself, without acknowledging that God presides over all.

Wicked governments and rulers have risen—and shall rise; nevertheless, God is on the throne governing everything (Rev. 17:17). Although sin is very real, God is actively governing the world. God did not just create the heavens and the earth and then step back to watch the world run by the laws of nature that He instituted. God is not a balcony observer, sitting on the sidelines, waiting to see what will happen. Rather, God continues to actively and sovereignly govern the world: "The king's heart is in the hand of the Lord, as the rivers of water: he turneth it whithersoever he will" (Prov. 21:1). Kings are ruled and overruled by Him (Eccles. 5:8).

God uses creatures as *second causes* to fulfill His will; He accomplishes His purpose through men and devils. He used the Egyptians to cause His people Israel to cry to Him for deliverance (Exod. 2—3). After being delivered from Egyptian bondage, Israel became disobedient. Then the Lord raised up the Assyrians to scourge the nation for its shortcomings (Isa. 10:5-6). God used wicked Shimei to chasten David to accomplish His purpose (II Sam. 16:5-13).

Satan and unbelievers are instruments used by God, but not to the extent that they are devoid of power to act for themselves. Men are motivated by their own plans. But their affections are wretchedly misplaced, and their actions manifest their inward conditions (Rom. 1:18-32). God enters into every second cause, but He does not cooperate in sin. God gives life (Acts 17:24-31) and sinners misuse the ability He gives them; this does not insinuate cooperation. A believer could never say, "I did that sinful act because God worked in me to will and to do that which is sinful."

Sustenance and *government* are two aspects of the one almighty and omnipresent God. All things are of, through, and to Him (Rom. 11:36). "For by him were all things created, that are in heaven, and that are in earth, visible and invisible, whether they be thrones, or dominions, or principalities, or powers: all things were created by him, and for him" (Col. 1:16). "A man's heart deviseth his way: but the Lord directeth his steps" (Prov. 16:9). "The Lord shall reign for ever . . ." (Ps. 146:10).

How can the two aspects of providence—God's sustenance and His government—leave room for human responsibility? In the Word of God both God's sovereignty and man's responsibility are taught. But divine revelation does not allow us to penetrate the mystery of the harmony between God's sovereignty and man's responsibility. Scripture always presents providence, the invincible power of God, *and* man's continual responsibility. The enemies of God are portrayed as enterprisers unable to escape God's supremacy. Although the enemies of the Lord Jesus Christ nailed Him to the cross, they did what God's disposing power had predetermined (Acts 2:23).

When we say, "God permits sin," we must be careful to clarify this. God does *not* allow the sinner to decide, free from His command. If He did, God would be merely an observer of a contest whose outcome is never certain. To sin or not to sin would ultimately lie in man's power of decision, and God could only react accordingly.

God's nonintervention is always a *positive* action, not helpless or frustrated inaction. However, positive providence does not make God the author of sin. Every act of sin is committed by a man whose life God sustains (Acts 17:28). Ananias and Sapphira were being sustained by God while they lied to Him (Acts 5:4). God restrained Abimelech from sinning against Sarah (Gen. 20:6), but He did not restrain David from sinning against Bathsheba and Uriah (II Sam. 11). Adam and many others were unrestrained, but God did restrain Laban from harming Jacob (Gen. 31:7) and prevented Balaam from cursing Israel (Num. 23).

God *suffers* (allows) sin to be committed. However, suffering is not connivance with, approbation of, or mere permission of sin. God not only allows men to walk in their own ways, He gives them up to uncleanness and vile affection and gives them over to a reprobate mind. He sends them strong delusions that they might believe a lie (II Thess. 2:11). God punishes sin with sin.

God may put things that are good in themselves in the way of persons. For instance, the law and the gospel become occasions for drawing out the corruptions of men's hearts. Paul said he would not have known sin but by the law (Rom. 7:7). The law and gospel themselves are good. However, the law draws corruption out of the heart, and the gospel becomes the savor of death to those who disbelieve (II Cor. 2:14-16).

God allows sin, but He sometimes overrules sin for good. He overruled Adam's sin for his perfection in grace. He overruled the sin of Joseph's brothers "to save much people alive . . ." (Gen. 50:20). He overruled the sin of the wicked men who crucified the Lord Jesus Christ and made His soul an offering for sin for the good of His elect (Isa. 53:11).

God is not responsible for man's sin (Isa. 45:7). He did not originate moral evil. Darkness did not proceed from God who is light, nor the evil of sin from God who is holy. Two contrasts appear in Isaiah 45:7—"I form the light, and create darkness: I make peace, and create evil: I the Lord do all these things." Light is contrasted with darkness, and peace is contrasted with evil. Darkness is the privation of light, and the evil of punishment is the privation of peace.

God forms light and creates darkness. He forms the light of nature and rational understanding. Every man who comes into the world possesses this light and understanding (John 1:9).

Darkness is also God's creature. Natural darkness results from the absence of the sun. Deprivation of divine light causes spiritual darkness.

Sin Decreed by the Forgiver

The Lord makes peace and creates evil (Isa. 45:7). He now makes peace among His saints. When Jesus Christ comes as King of kings and Lord of lords, He will make universal peace. The Lord announced through Isaiah that He would remove the peace the Israelites were enjoying and send them the evil of punishment for their sins.

For the evil that God creates is the evil of *punishment for sin*, not the evil of sin itself. Sin is not found among God's creatures in Genesis 1. Sin did not begin with God's original creation. The Lord does not infuse any evil into men. Rather, He subjects depraved men to various providential dealings; He allows sin and overrules it for the good of His people.

Sin began among the angelic host with Lucifer and with mankind it began in Adam. God purposed the fall of both. If He had not, neither could have fallen. The Lord also purposed to prepare redemption for His elect through the sacrifice of the Lord Jesus Christ. Although evil hands were associated with the preparation of that redemptive work, those wicked hands were only instruments that God used to fulfill His purpose. *God* made Christ's soul an offering for sin: "Yet it pleased the *Lord* to bruise him; *he* hath put him to grief: when thou shalt make his soul an offering for sin, he shall see his seed, he shall prolong his days, and the pleasure of the Lord shall prosper in his hand" (Isa. 53:10).

We must distinguish between the words *purpose* and *author*. God purposed sin; otherwise, it could not exist. According to God's determinate counsel and foreknowledge, the sins of wicked men nailed the Lord Jesus Christ to the cross (Acts 2:23). God purposed to order events so that evil should come to pass to fulfill His eternal purpose. Nevertheless, He hates evil. To say that God is the author of sin—that is, the agent, actor, or doer of a wicked thing—would be blasphemy. Sin had no actual existence before it was committed by creatures whom God pronounced *good* after His act of

19

creating them. Therefore, sin's beginning cannot be attributed to God.

God's foreknowledge of sin does not make Him the author of sin; *anticipated* sin and *actual* sin are entirely different. Just as divine election or foreordination does not cause one's actual redemption, so foreknowledge of sin's occurrence does not cause that sin.

Sin became a reality only as God's creatures perverted His will. It has no original substance in itself. Sin has no thesis. It has only antithesis. Since sin came by God's creatures, it is a secondary and not a primary consideration.

People seek to excuse their own sin by asking, "Why did God make Adam capable of falling?" They refuse to admit a personal sinful condition. For that reason, considering the origin of sin is not as innocent as it may appear.

God created man capable of falling because He could make him in no other condition. God cannot create God. Whatever He creates must be inferior to Himself. Man was created upright (Eccles. 7:29), but he was created with two principles: *inferior* and *superior*. The inferior principle was related to man's flesh, and the superior principle was related to his fellowship with God. When Adam fell, he lost the superior principle and retained the inferior (which had become corrupted). Adam could no longer fellowship with God, so he fled to the wilderness, seeking to hide himself from God. The inferior principle became the reigning principle in the lives of Adam and his descendants. When the superior principle was forfeited through sin, man was alienated from the life of God. Every person since Adam comes into the world dead in trespasses and sins.

Adam's trial was ordained of God because probation is an essential part of self-determination. However, God's ordination of Adam's trial was benevolent, not unjust. And God provided hope for Adam and all His elect ones.

The Lord Jesus Christ could never be tempted the same way as Adam was. He had no inferior principle, no weakness within, to yield to temptation. He had only the divine principle—He could not yield to external temptation. Temptation itself cannot pervert the soul. Only an evil will, self-determined against God, can turn temptation into an occasion for ruin.

Satan was the first actor in sin and the first tempter to sin. When he approached Eve, he concealed the fact of his own fall and his enmity against God. Sin began with Lucifer. God pronounced it evil (Ezek. 28:15).

If Adam, who possessed the strength of uprightness, yielded to temptation, how can Adam's descendants, who possess only an inferior principle, resist it? All men react in only one way until God's grace intervenes. None can overcome temptation apart from the grace of God.

2

The Necessity of
God's Forgiveness

Sin's beginning has a character that is qualitatively different from that of all origins. Only one verse in the Bible speaks of its exact source: "Thou wast perfect in thy ways from the day that thou wast created, till iniquity was found in thee" (Ezek. 28:15). Chapter 14 of Isaiah should be studied with Ezekiel 28. Both chapters deal with Lucifer and his fall.

Some interpret Ezekiel 28 by applying it to only the king of Tyrus. The prophet *was* speaking of a particular king, but it was Lucifer who directed that wicked king. Two verses (vs. 13, 15) refute the idea that this portion of Scripture refers primarily to the king of Tyrus. The king of Tyrus was not a *created* person. He came into the world by *generation*. Scripture goes beyond him to speak of Lucifer, who became Satan.

Adam fell when he was tempted in the garden of Eden. Sin, then, began in the human family in the garden of Eden. However, sin actually had its beginning in Lucifer, the son of the morning (Isa. 14).

Lucifer was finitely, not infinitely, perfect until iniquity was found in him (Ezek. 28:15). Finite perfection is capable of sinning; whereas, infinite perfection is incapable of sinning. Infinite perfection belongs to God alone. "Till iniquity was found in thee" (Ezek. 28:15) is the only statement in the Bible concerning the origin of sin. Every other reference to sin only amplifies this statement.

The primary difference between Lucifer's and Adam's sin is that Lucifer's sin originated solely within himself, without any evil outside himself. Adam, however, was enticed from without. He had a weakness within himself to respond to temptation. Since sin came into the world, it is the motive for all man's thoughts and actions. Each man must see himself in complete solidarity with Adam, recognizing sin as his own. Not until then will he genuinely confess.

Sin is the biggest of all contradictions. It affects all things. However, God uses it in the ways of righteousness and justice as an instrument of His own glory. Nevertheless God does not tolerate sin; He condemns it.

There is an unusual relation between seeking to know the origin of sin and an exculpation of one's own guilt. That search is not as innocent as it might appear, for the motive may be to blame another. Sin must be considered as one's own. No genuine confession of sin will be made by a person so long as he looks for sin's origin. It is only when one recognizes his sin that he cries for forgiveness.

Sin began neither with God's creation of Lucifer and the angelic host nor with His original creation of man. Sin is related to reality's destruction and disruption, whether with Lucifer's fall or with Adam's fall in the garden of Eden. The reality of sin can never be assigned to the goodness of God in creation. All things God created were pronounced *good* (Gen. 1).

Sin took place as an event. Anyone who says God made man sinful denies the holiness and love of God. The person who says that moral purity is man's goal instead of his starting point attributes to God the principle condemned by Paul: "Let us do evil, that good may come . . ." (Rom. 3:8). Sin is man's fall, not his exaltation. It is his disgrace, not his dignity.

Satan subtly lured Eve and then Eve tempted Adam. Satan deceived Eve by making her believe that God had withheld something from her. The devil continues to use the same technique, making people believe that God has deprived them of something.

Eve's reaction to Satan's temptation is common among mankind. She allowed Satan to subtract from, add to, alter, and misapply the word of God (Gen. 3:1-6; [cf. 2:16-17; 3:4, 5; II Peter 3:16; II Tim. 2:15]). Because Eve's tragic mistakes are followed by all men in all ages, Satan's methods of tempting men to sin have never changed. Eve responded to Satan's persuasion and sought higher knowledge. Instead of finding it, she lost her good knowledge and fellowship with God. Then she persuaded her husband and he did likewise.

Freedom was God's gift to Adam, and Adam's abuse of that freedom was his sin. When he fell, every man without exception became enslaved. Does man have the ability to choose? Yes! However, he freely chooses evil in the same manner that a motorless automobile chooses to run downhill or Niagara Falls chooses to go only one direction—down.

Adam's original uprightness was not achieved by his own ability. God gave it to him when He created him. Adam's original position before God meant that he bore within himself the possibility but not the actuality of sin and death.

Man is a sinner (Rom. 1:18-32). His ungodly, unrighteous, depraved condition prevents his standing in the presence of the righteous, holy God. Man needs righteousness. Since none are righteous, a righteousness must be provided by the Lord to meet human need.

The objective revelation of God in nature is sufficient to render every man under heaven inexcusable before God (Rom. 1:19-20). No man is righteous (Rom. 3:10). All are under the wrath of God.

God's wrath stands in apparent antithesis to His righteousness. However, God's justice is retributive in reference to sin; the wrath of God is a *principle*, not a passion. Wrath and love are complementary attributes in God. The wrath of God differs from the wrath existing in a man. No man outside of Jesus Christ has perfect hatred. In man, wrath is an exciting passion. In God, it is a principle which makes no ripple on the infinite rivers of His holy Being. In man, wrath is a malignant passion, burning with the desire to make its object miserable. With God, wrath is the natural reaction of divine justice—God has no evil disposition. In man, wrath is a selfish passion. In God, it is an unselfish principle. In man, wrath is a painful passion. In God, wrath is a necessary principle.

One could neither esteem nor love God if He viewed honesty and dishonesty, cruelty and benevolence alike. The truth that wrath is as much a part of God's character as love is emphasizes three important points: (1) It corrects the theological error that Christ's death appeased divine vengeance. According to the Word of God, Christ's death was the effect, not the cause, of God's love and wrath. God loved His own in Christ before the foundation of the world. The effect of that love was that He sent His Son to die on the cross of Calvary for all whom the Father gave Him in the covenant of redemption. (2) It supplies a terrible warning to sinners—"Be sure your sins will find you out." All sin shall be brought to light. (3) It urges the necessity for regeneration. The only way to avoid God's wrath is to avoid sin. The only way to avoid sin is through the redemptive work of Jesus Christ which is applied by the Holy Spirit in regeneration.

All men, even the unsaved, have some principles; but they do not abide by them. God is His own principle, His own law. Arbitrariness cannot be attributed to Him. He is His own standard.

God's wrath is *perpetually revealed.* Fear of God's wrath caused our first parents to flee God's presence (Gen. 3:8). The same fear caused Judas to hang himself.

Conscience has compelled many to reveal secret sins, although no torture could extort such confessions. God's wrath is perpetually revealed in the general, moral sentiment of mankind.

The perpetual revelation of God's wrath is *preparatory* and *predictive*. In Romans 1:18, "reveal" means to uncover, bring to light; hence, to make known. Something is revealed when it becomes known by its effect. Thus, the thought of the heart is revealed in an expression from man. That which proceeds from the heart reveals man's character.

The human race has always had an indwelling sense of God's justice. All men know the righteous judgment of God. Consequently, they know that those who practice sin are worthy of death. They know there is a righteous wrath against sin (Rom. 1:32). The repentant malefactor suspended on the cross acknowledged that his punishment was just (Luke 23:39-41).

All sin is against God. Men will continue to commit sin against the sovereign God until the last enemy is destroyed. Sin against an individual is actually against God. All unrighteousness is sin (I John 5:17), and whatever is not of faith is sin (Rom. 14:23).

"Ungodliness" denotes irreverence for God, and pertains to man's religious character; "unrighteousness" denotes that which is immoral. Ungodliness has no fear of God (Rom. 3:18); unrighteousness has no standard for man. Ungodliness denies God's character. (Anyone who claims that Jesus Christ was peccable denies the holy character of the blessed Lord.) Unrighteousness, which is injustice, destroys man's character. Ungodliness attacks the Godhead. Unrighteousness attacks God's government. Ungodliness condemns God. Unrighteousness seeks to justify man.

The doctrine of sin is discussed in Romans 1:18-32. Sin must always be considered in its relation to God's sovereignty and providence. When God gives people up, He does not simply permit them to stray from Him.

Romans 1:24 speaks of God's positive withdrawal. God withdraws all restraint. He does not infuse any new evil principle; those who continue to pursue evil fulfill that which is already in their hearts.

He who commits sin transgresses the law: "Whosoever committeth sin transgresseth also the law: for sin is the transgression of the law" (I John 3:4). God's standard is His holy law, and He is His own law. Sin and redemption go hand in hand. They stand or fall together. Because of sin, God provided redemption for His people. Sin and redemption become measurements of each other. When sin is minimized, redemption automatically becomes impoverished. God's law is the only standard for measurement.

Sin, defined best by the phrase "missing the mark," obviously exists. Its existence can be proved by the revelation of Scripture, and it can also be verified apart from any knowledge of the Word of God. God reveals sin to men by the Holy Scriptures, Jesus Christ, and general revelation. The unclean lives lived by men today are the result of their turning from the light unveiled in creation.

Death did not exist until Adam's fall in the garden of Eden. Death is the consequence of sin: "Wherefore, as by one man sin entered into the world, and death by sin; and so death passed upon all men, for that all have sinned" (Rom. 5:12). The whole creation groans because it is under God's wrath. Every person who dies manifests the reality of sin.

Sin is sinful because it is unlike God who is holy. God describes sin as *transgression* in that it oversteps His boundaries; as *iniquity* in that it is altogether wrong; as *sin* in that it misses the mark; as *error* in that it disregards light and goes astray; as *wickedness* in that it lacks fear of God; as *evil* because it opposes all things of God; as *disobedience* because it is unwilling to be guided by God's will; as *unbelief* in that it fails to trust God; as *lawlessness* because it has contempt for divine law; and

28

as *universal* since none is exempt. All have sinned (Rom. 3:23). Everyone has always been a sinner. Each one sinned in Adam. There is solidarity of mankind in Adam's fall in the garden of Eden. Sin is a fact, an obvious reality. The knowledge of sin comes by the law (Rom. 3:20). Salvation comes only through righteousness provided by God (Rom. 3:21).

Man's coming short of God's glory (Rom. 3:23) issues from his fallen condition. *Falling short* denotes the sinful habit—an act flowing from the fall. When men fall short, they do not value God's name or His attributes. They value themselves above God and exchange His truth for a lie.

Overwhelming data proves that man is a fallen creature. Every person has some sense of rightness and wrongness: "Therefore thou art inexcusable, O man, whosoever thou art that judgest: for wherein thou judgest another, thou condemnest thyself; for thou that judgest doest the same things" (Rom. 2:1). A person must have a sense of right and wrong in order to judge another's actions.

Man's confused drives, urges, and impulses demonstrate that he is fallen. Before the fall, those forces in Adam were perfectly balanced. His desire for food, love, and self-preservation before the fall were harmonious. However, when he fell, they were contaminated with sin, perverted, and corrupted. Since then, man's drive for food, for self-preservation, and his urge for love are unbalanced.

Sin is a fact, whether it is dormant like a slumbering volcano or evidenced in the devastating lava of a man's fiery passions. Sin is there, and the evil nature of an individual will at times manifest itself in the hot lava of thoughts and deeds.

The reality of sin has many witnesses. The *law* of God was given to uncover the fact of sin (Rom. 3:20). The law is a standard to measure man's shortcomings. It is the scale on which man must weigh his deficiency, a looking glass which shows man his sinfulness, a stethoscope which shows the condition of man's heart, a rule which evidences man's crookedness, an officer which demands man's condemnation, and a judge that condemns man to death for his disobedience.

Scripture, the highest court of appeal, declares the fact of sin. Sin is a grievous malady (Gen. 18:20), contaminating the whole man. Isaiah described man as rotten from the top of his head to the bottom of his feet (Isa. 1:5-6). Sin is an obscuring cloud that hides the face of God from man (Isa. 59:2). It is a crouching beast (Gen. 4:7). It is a binding cord (Prov. 5:22), a rest destroyer. Sin is a written record, an accusing witness (Isa. 59:12). Sin is a sum of addition—sin added to sin.

The coming of Jesus Christ also reveals the fact of sin. During the personal ministry of the Lord, many of His followers confessed their sin as they beheld His holiness. Just as a revelation of God's holiness in the Old Testament caused saints to confess their sins (Isa. 6:5; Dan. 9:5), New Testament saints recognized their sin when in the presence of Christ and confessed it. (Men like Pharaoh, Balaam, and Judas also confessed their sin, but they did not manifest repentance.)

Sin is a state of delusion and deception. It is not merely a deed. There can be no act apart from principle, and sin is the *source* from which the act proceeds. Sin is a quality of being. There is no sin separated from a sinner, and there is no act apart from an actor. The fact that man sins verifies that he is a sinner. One who knows what he should do and does not do it reveals that he is a sinner (James 4:17). In that case, the act of sin is not involved; his disobedient heart proves he sinned. Although his sin is not manifested, it comes from the source or principle of his being.

Sin is a state of the heart (Jer. 17:9). Sin that cannot be known by men is not a sin of action. Many sins are committed of which others are unaware—they are committed in the heart. Sin exists in the soul prior to one's consciousness of it. Paul said sin lay dormant in his heart until the commandment came, causing him to become conscious of sin lying within (Rom. 7:9). A momentary act of sin cannot dwell or reign in the heart, but the principle of sin does.

Sin covers its deepest intentions while it masquerades as good. The goal of every sin is to deceive, and sin's penalty is death: "For the wages of sin is death; but the gift of God is eternal life through Jesus Christ our Lord" (Rom. 6:23). There are three kinds of death: physical, spiritual, and eternal. The element of *separation* is common to all three. Physical death is separation of the soul from the body. Spiritual death is separation of the soul from God. Eternal death is separation of both soul and body from God throughout eternity.

There are three kinds of life: physical, spiritual, and eternal. The element of *union* is common to all three. Physical life is union of the soul with the body. Spiritual life is union of the soul with God. Eternal life is union of both soul and body with God throughout eternity.

Faith does not flee responsibility, and it never explains guilt in any way but proceeding from man's own depraved heart. The sun causes a foul odor to proceed from a dunghill, but it does not cause the dunghill. It is only the occasion for drawing forth the scent. The Lord forced Pharaoh to an issue, causing him to manifest the hardness of his heart. God was not the author of his hardness; He only left him to his own unrestrained, depraved nature. People react in the same manner to the proclaimed truth of God's Word—it becomes the occasion for them to manifest their depraved natures. Hence, man's condition before God proves the necessity for forgiveness of his sin by God.

3

God's Everlasting Forgiveness

The three aspects to God's forgiveness of sinners whom He has elected to salvation are (1) *everlasting* forgiveness, (2) *restorative* forgiveness, and (3) *governmental* forgiveness. Everlasting forgiveness occurs at regeneration. Restorative forgiveness is related to those who are everlastingly forgiven—every person saved by the grace of God needs continual cleansing. Governmental forgiveness is for the children of God who have sinned and been restored to fellowship.

Every person's condition outside of Jesus Christ is described in Ephesians 2:1-3. Nevertheless, God intervenes and everlastingly forgives those He elected to salvation: "But God, who is rich in mercy, for his great love wherewith he loved us, even when we were dead in sins, hath quickened us together with Christ, (by grace ye are saved;)" (Eph. 2:4-5). The foundation for that forgiveness is the blood of Jesus Christ (Eph. 1:7).

David, a child of God, cried to the Lord for restorative forgiveness, recognizing that none can stand in the presence of the Lord if God marks iniquities (Ps. 130:3). "But there is forgiveness with thee . . ." (Ps. 130:4). Note, however, that sin is not necessarily done with when it is confessed and when the sinner is restoratively forgiven. David yielded to his flesh when he com-

33

mitted sin with Bathsheba and had Uriah killed; therefore, he experienced *governmental forgiveness.* The
sword never departed from his house (II Sam. 12:10).
Just so, even though the blood of Jesus Christ cleanses
from all sin, if a person sows to the flesh, he shall reap
corruption. "For he that soweth to his flesh shall of the
flesh reap corruption; but he that soweth to the Spirit
shall of the Spirit reap life everlasting" (Gal. 6:8).

The Lord Jesus has the power to forgive sin. He spoke
to the palsied man, saying, "thy sins be forgiven thee"
(Mark 2:5). The scribes knew that God alone could forgive sin, but they did not recognize the deity of Jesus
Christ (vs. 6-7). It is beautifully appropriate that the
designation *Son of man* is used in this passage: "the Son
of man hath power on earth to forgive sins . . ." (v. 10).
The Savior has power to forgive sin not only as the Son
of God but as the Son of man who came to be the
Surety of the elect. The eternal Son of God assumed a
human nature and was given the title "Son of man." He
was more than *a* son of man. He was *the* Son of man.
"Him hath God exalted . . . a Prince and a Saviour, for
to give repentance to Israel, and forgiveness of sins"
(Acts 5:31). Jesus Christ does not set the sinner free by
a simple exercise of His own authority. That would
violate obligations of law and demands of justice and
holiness. The Lord Jesus Christ paid the penalty for sin.
He fulfilled the law and satisfied justice and holiness.

The scribes accused the Lord of blasphemy (Mark
2:7) because they did not recognize that He was
the eternal Son of God. But because Jesus Christ is the
mediator between God and man, He was not blasphe-
mous. Had He not been divine, their accusation would
have been true. To help men make the staggering equa-
tion between the Man Jesus Christ and the Godhead,
Christ performed a miracle to prove He was the God-
Man.

Some erroneously interpret John 20:23: "Whose
soever sins ye remit, they are remitted unto them; and

whose soever sins ye retain, they are retained." They believe it teaches that some men have power to forgive sin. One must observe from the context of that verse that the Lord was addressing His disciples before the Holy Spirit came in His abiding presence on the day of Pentecost. The disciples were not given power to *effectually* or *authoritatively* remit sin; they could only *declaratively* remit it. No man has ever had power to effectually or authoritatively pardon sin. God alone can do that. Under the law, the priest only *pronounced* a cleansed leper clean. The priest was God's representative on earth to declare that God had cleansed the leper. Likewise, New Testament ministers only pronounce that a penitent believer's sins have been forgiven by the sovereign God.

Divine forgiveness is the *eternal, immutable* plan of God. It is not an act of excited sympathy. Man's forgiveness, on the other hand, is generally excited by sympathy for the offender.

Divine forgiveness is *irreversible*, without limitation. Every sin a Christian shall commit is abundantly pardoned by the Lord. Contrasted to this, man's forgiveness is limited; it is not an irreversible plan.

Divine forgiveness occurs *within* a believer—grace works a change in his heart. Man's forgiveness, however, is outside an offender.

When God forgives, He *forgets* the forgiven man's sin. Forgetfulness with man is a defect; however, with God it is an attribute. God never compares His forgiveness with human forgiveness. Scripture states instead that He puts the forgiven person's sin behind His back, as far as the east is from the west, and casts the sin into the depths of the sea (Ps. 103:12; Isa. 38:17; Mic. 7:19). Divine forgiveness so far excels human forgiveness that no human analogy can illustrate it.

Nonremembrance of sin implies forgiveness thereof: "their sins and their iniquities will I remember no more" (Heb. 8:12). God's forgiveness is so complete that He describes it as not remembering the forgiven man's sin, iniquities, and transgressions. With Him forgiveness is tantamount to forgetting a person's sin. He does not store remembrance of it in His mind; He does not think over the sins of His people. Their iniquity is removed, and the righteous Judge has no judicial memory of it.

Man, however, exercises his memory to meditate on things laid up in his mind. He may almost have forgotten a certain thing, but then some incident occurs and recalls the event to his mind.

Divine forgiveness signifies that God will never seek any further atonement. "Now where remission of these is, there is no more offering for sin" (Heb. 10:18). God will never again punish what He has already punished. What He has forgotten cannot be remembered.

Those who do not hold to the biblical theology say that *any* father would forgive his child. That statement is based on a misunderstood and misapplied concept of the fatherhood of God and the brotherhood of man. Two flaws are apparent in this liberal view. First of all, God is not the Father of all sinning, wicked rebels. Second, God is more than the creative Father of individuals.

A private being may forgive private wrong irrespective of the settlement of judgment. However, God is the great public Governor of the universe. Sin against His government cannot be forgiven apart from sacrifice. Forgiveness does not indicate remission of punishment. Jesus Christ was punished in the place of those elected in Him. He became Surety for those the Father gave Him in the covenant of redemption.

Every recipient of grace knows that God's forgiveness is that of reconciliation. Scriptures do not state that God forgives because He is loving and merciful. They testify that He is faithful and just, and He forgives on that basis. God's justice must be satisfied, and it is satisfied in the person of the Lord Jesus Christ. God forgives in love because He pardons in justice.

Gracious forgiveness harmonizes with the *wrath* of the Sovereign. Sin must be punished, and God's wrath must be poured out. Jesus Christ was made an offering for sin; He stood in the *place* of sinners, bearing their just punishment.

Gracious forgiveness harmonizes with the *love* of the Holy Father. Since justice was satisfied in Christ's sacrifice, love can be extended to God's chosen ones, and mercy can operate to bring them to Christ.

The Greek verb for *forgiveness* signifies a sending forth or a sending away. The Greek noun indicates dismissal or release. Divine forgiveness enables the believer to know, with full assurance of faith, that his sins are forgiven. Abraham, David, and Hezekiah are three Old Testament saints who knew their sins were everlastingly forgiven (see Rom. 4; Ps. 32; Isa. 38).

In the same way every repentant sinner can know that his sins have been forgiven. The grace of God reigns, and the riches of grace are displayed in divine forgiveness. It is absolutely perfect. The following make it so: (1) The repentant sinner is *fully* forgiven. (2) He is *freely* forgiven. (3) He is *everlastingly* forgiven. (4) The forgiveness *extends to all* for whom Christ died. (5) Forgiveness is *by faith*, without any conditions performed by the sinner. (6) It is absolutely *irreversible*. A sinner who knows he has been everlastingly forgiven will avoid antinomianism. He desires to please God and not himself.

4

God's Restorative Forgiveness

I JOHN 1:7—2:2
ZECHARIAH 3:1-10

God's restorative forgiveness of sin is necessary for every person born of the Spirit. The blood of the Lord Jesus Christ is *efficacious* to cleanse God's chosen ones from all sin. "But if we walk in the light, as he is in the light, we have fellowship one with another, and the blood of Jesus Christ his Son cleanseth us from all sin" (I John 1:7). Christ's blood is not only *competent* to forgive a person's sin but it *continually* cleanses him from all sin—past, present, and future. All the sins of believers were future when Jesus Christ died on the cross. He atoned for them when He became the sinner's substitute, for His blood has cleansing property. His death was objective—it judicially put away sin from before the Lord. If His blood had been incompetent to atone for all sin, believers could not plead the mercy of God.

The Word of God shows that justification and sanctification are so bound together that they cannot be separated. Justification does precede sanctification, that is, the sins of the believer were judicially atoned for in Christ's death. Sanctification is God's work in the believer to make him suitable for God's presence. What Jesus Christ *objectively* wrought on the cross, the Holy Spirit *subjectively* applies to the hearts of believers.

Hence, there is an *initial* cleansing, and there is a *continual* cleansing. The tear ducts of the eye are a good example. In the same way, the blood of Christ is always there, continually cleansing the redeemed sinner from impurities that intrude.

The prophet Zechariah taught restorative forgiveness; Jesus Christ's advocacy is portrayed in chapter 3. The Holy Spirit's message to Joshua the priest, who was a representative to Israel, proceeded from cleansing to obedience to service. Joshua (Jeshua) was one of the priests among the exiles who returned to Babylon with Zerubbabel (Ezra 2:36-39). The dirty garments in which he was clothed signified Israel's despicable state at that time. Israel needed restorative forgiveness. Even the priesthood had become defiled and unsuited for holy service. The prophet Malachi described Israel's priests as a sad contrast to the original priesthood represented by Phinehas (Num. 25).

Joshua stood before the Lord (Zech. 3:1). A sense of shame is more acute when one stands in God's presence. In the world's twilight, much may pass unnoticed which in the light of God must be condemned. Everything is open to the Lord (Heb. 4:13). When the white light of God's presence shines upon a Christian, he cries with Job, "If I wash myself with snow water, and make my hands never so clean: yet shalt thou plunge me in the ditch, and mine own clothes shall abhor me" (Job 9:30-31). God is holy; therefore, no one can stand before Him and declare himself clean. The more a person knows about the Lord, the more he loathes himself and repents. Restorative forgiveness is necessary every day of one's life.

Satan stood at Joshua's right hand to resist him (Zech. 3:1). The devil stands beside *every* child of God to resist and accuse him. He seeks to prevent him from doing the will of God. Then, when the believer fails, Satan accuses him before the Lord. Nevertheless, the Lord Jesus Christ is the Christian's Advocate. He sits at the right hand of the Father and stands to plead the believer's case; Christians stand in Him who represents them to the Father.

The Lord rebuked Satan and reminded him that He had chosen Israel. He chose them for His loves (Song of Sol. 7:12) and manifested His love to them. Israel was a "brand plucked out of the fire"—a figurative expression of the punishment Israel had endured in Babylonian captivity. They had been disobedient, the Lord had chastened them, and then delivered them. It stands to reason that God had not delivered Israel from Egypt or from Babylon to destroy them.

All believers were chosen in Christ before the foundation of the world. There is a sense in which they too are plucked from the fire of judgment when the Lord calls them out from the people of the world (I Peter 1:2). He also delivers them from punishment for sin they commit after they are saved. But sin removes the enjoyment of the promises of God. Christians with unconfessed sin cannot enjoy God's promises or blessings; until they confess their sin they are not restored to fellowship.

Jesus Christ offered Himself once in the end of the age to put away sin (Heb. 9:26). No additional propitiation is necessary to forgive the believer who has been everlastingly forgiven. Christ died to put away sin's penalty *from* the elect. He lives to put away sins *from within* the elect. Christ's death on the cross destroyed sin's penalty *for* believers. The ever-living Christ destroys sin's power *over* believers (Rom. 5:6-10).

Both everlasting and restorative forgiveness are taught in Romans 5:10—"For if, when we were enemies, we were reconciled to God by the death of his Son, much more, being reconciled, we shall be saved by his life." Everlasting forgiveness must be associated with reconciliation. The person who has been everlastingly forgiven has been reconciled to the Father, and saved by Christ's life. The sinner is forgiven in *justification*. The saint is forgiven in *sanctification*.

41

Sin cannot make its way into God's presence. Jesus Christ prevents that. If it were possible for a person's sin to enter God's presence, that person would be banished in judgment. Sin does make its way into the believer's presence, causing him to lose fellowship with the Lord and severing the joy of his salvation. Enjoyment of the things of the Lord is experienced through restorative forgiveness. Sin in the believer's life affects his thoughts about God and sin. He begins to look lightly on sin and loses sight of the holiness of God.

Christians desire not to sin. When they do sin, they should avoid despair (Gal. 6:1) for Jesus Christ is their Advocate. They are kept *safe* by Christ's advocacy, and they are kept in *fellowship* by confession. A Christian's failure to confess sin hinders the testimony of both the Christian and the church: "He that covereth his sins shall not prosper: but whoso confesseth and forsaketh them shall have mercy" (Prov. 28:13). Nothing can hinder a Christian's *standing* in the Lord; his *state*, however, is imperfect. He should pray with profound sincerity that the Lord forgive his trespasses. He needs to reflect on his abiding need for cleansing from all sin by Christ's blood.

Jesus Christ *cleanses* the believer from all sin. Not one of a Christian's sin can enter God's presence; Jesus Christ is there pleading His own merit. Satan stands at the believer's side. He does his work at the court of conscience, at the bar of public opinion. However, he also appears before the divine Judge. The believer's Advocate rebukes Satan, alleges God's election, and points to the believer as a trophy of divine mercy.

Every time a Christian sins, Christ's blood is there to cleanse him. Conversely, sins of unbelievers are credited to their accounts. All the sins they commit are treasured up for punishment (Rom. 2:5). When unbelievers stand before the Lord at the great white throne judgment, all those sins will be reviewed and judged by the wrath of God.

5

Advocacy Required for Restorative Forgiveness

The Lord Jesus Christ is Advocate not for sin but for *sinners saved by grace.* (Technically, God cannot forgive *sin.*) John's first epistle was written to Christians to assure them of their position in Christ and God's provision for them. The problems presented by John were more than individual. They dealt not only with the penalty of sin but with fellowship in the family of God. The solution is in Him who was from the beginning.

The apostle John declared the eternity of Christ in his gospel—Jesus Christ was *in* the beginning (John 1:1). In his first epistle, John emphasized that Christ was *from* the beginning (1:1). This epistle asserts the manifestation of the eternal Christ in time. The context shows that John heard, saw, looked upon, and handled the Son of God. That was possible only in time, not in eternity. Hence, he proclaimed that the eternal Son of God was before the beginning and He was manifested in time for His elect. In time He came, died, rose, and became Advocate.

The Word of Life is *eternal, historical, personal,* and *social.* Eternal Life existed before the beginning of time. Jesus Christ was before the heavens and earth were created, and He was manifested in time. This Life was also historical. Christ was heard with physical ears and

43

seen with physical eyes. The apostles actually beheld Him. Christians today meditate upon Him. The apostles handled Him. Christians enjoy intimate fellowship with Him.

Jesus Christ was manifested in the *past* on earth for the salvation of the elect. He is manifested in the *present* in heaven for their sanctification. He shall be manifested in the *future* for their glorification. The sin problem in I John is *sanctification* rather than *justification*. Christ's death dealt with the *judicial* aspect of sin. His life deals with the *practical* aspect of sin. Sanctification involves the advocacy of Jesus Christ.

The Life was manifested; consequently, the elect who have been brought to the knowledge of their salvation manifest that Life which flows through them. A true witness of Jesus Christ has been enabled by God-given faith to see Christ. He then shows Jesus Christ in his life. God is light for the believer's walk (I John 1:5).

Jesus Christ offered Himself once to put away sin. He will never offer Himself again. He lives as the Advocate for the believer, not the unbeliever. He is Intercessor for believers. The identity of a lawyer in an earthly court is of no peculiar consequence. That is not true in the heavenly court. The Lord Jesus Christ is the believer's Lawyer, pleading His own righteousness before the holy, righteous Father.

Christ has a vital interest in His own clients. He became their Surety, shedding His blood for their redemption. After their reconciliation by His blood, He represents them before the Father. No man has a place in God's court. He is already guilty before God: "For there is not a just man upon earth, that doeth good, and sinneth not" (Eccles. 7:20). His case is lost.

Christ's Advocacy manifests both the Christian's *failure* and his *security*. All Christians sin. To do so is to walk in spiritual darkness. (The word *darkness* is used in seven different ways in Scripture.) In I John 1:6, it is not natural darkness that is referred to but a failure to walk according to truth. A Christian does not habitually pursue a course of darkness. However, he does walk in darkness when he backslides. Sinless perfection in this life is impossible, for the old sin nature has not yet been eradicated.

An essential characteristic of an advocate is that he must be the *uncompromising friend of the government.* Jesus Christ is such a friend to God's holy law (government). Human lawyers may yield to pressure, money, or some other human persuasion. Contrarily, the Christian's Advocate yields not one iota. He never falters, fails, or changes.

Another fundamental property of an advocate is that he must be the *undeviating friend of the dishonored law.* Jesus Christ fulfilled every letter of the law. He alone is qualified for advocacy for Christians. Human lawyers seek ways of ignoring broken law or misrepresenting the contents of the law. Christ honors the law. To dishonor it would be to dishonor Himself because it is His law.

A qualifier for advocacy must be *inherently righteous;* and Jesus Christ, the Son of God, is clear of complicity in any of the crimes of the sinner.

One who is equipped for advocacy must be the *compassionate friend of the sinner.* Jesus Christ proves that He possesses that attribute. He died for the believer, became his Surety, and intercedes in his behalf, all of which manifests His compassion for the sinner.

A suitable advocate willingly *volunteers gratuitous service.* Jesus Christ has already paid the price on Calvary, and He charges the believer nothing for His service.

A *good plea* is vital to advocacy. The believer's Advocate pleads His own character, which is righteousness. Jesus loved the elect and voluntarily took an interest in them. The Just One proved His interest by becoming the Substitute for unjust ones. Christ the Anointed One has the authority to plead the believer's case. Jesus Christ the righteous demonstrates His plea.

45

Christ's advocacy supposes four things: (1) There is an offender. (Christians offend every day). (2) There is an accuser. Satan seeks to prevent Christians from performing the will of God, and when they fall, he accuses them before God. (3) There is a Judge. God is the righteous Judge. (4) There is a defense. Jesus Christ is the Defender. Christ's advocacy declares that believers are sorry creatures; only the grace of God within them is worthy. Christ's advocacy is required to keep believers clean. God has well provided for them: blood to wash, Priest to intercede, and Advocate to plead.

No new sacrifice is made by the Advocate—Jesus Christ does not offer Himself for sin. He does not die for sin, and the salvation of no one is obtained. Saved ones are *kept safe* through advocacy. He sanctifies them in that office. As Savior, He obtained eternal redemption for the elect. As Advocate, He maintains their right thereto.

Christ's priesthood differs from His advocacy:

PRIEST	ADVOCATE
He sits.	He stands pleading.
He is merciful and faithful.	He is faithful and just.
He represents infirm believers before the Father.	He is there to help believers when they sin.
He gives grace to sustain believers.	He represents sinning believers.
He gives grace to help in the time of need.	He helps believers in times of sin.
Believers approach Him boldly.	Believers approach Him humbly, confessing their sin.
He ever lives to make intercession for believers.	He pleads His own death on the cross.
He goes before believers, interceding, praying.	He comes after believers, after they have sinned, pleading their case.

Advocacy Required for Restorative Forgiveness

Advocates among men frequently deny allegations brought against their clients. Jesus Christ admits those brought against His clients. Advocates among men, if they admit the charge, often seek to justify it Christ pleads no excuse for believers. They are guilty, but He pleads His own merit. Lawyers among men undertake their work not from love for justice or humanity but for personal considerations. Christ has in mind the glory of God. He is concerned about glorifying God's justice. Too many lawyers are concerned about personal achievement. Advocates among men seek to influence the minds of adjudicators. Jesus Christ does not influence the Father—He knows all. Christ influences His clients. Lawyers among men sometimes relinquish their briefs to protect their self-respect and reputation. Jesus Christ is never taken by surprise. He knows all about His clients; therefore, His briefs are never relinquished.

6

God's Character
Revealed by
Restorative Forgiveness

John's first epistle declares that God is light, love, and life. There are two facets of divine revelation in this epistle. The joy of God is love, and the judgment of God is light. Judgment and joy are not contradictory. John emphasized three major truths concerning *light* (I John 1:5—2:2): (1) Light depicts God's character. (2) God's light shines into the hearts of His elect to regenerate them. (3) God's light reveals sin in the lives of Christians.

1. *Light depicts God's character:* ". . . God is light . . ." (I John 1:5). John did not state that He is *a* light or *the* light but that He *is* light. The Lord is the *source* of all light. In Him there is absolute light. Absolute light makes known to men God's being and nature. God is light without darkness. Hence, John positively and negatively described God's character.

Light is *self-manifested.* Men see by means of light, but they do not see light itself. God too is invisible. Light is *transparent.* Transparency describes the purity of God's character. Light is *unchanging.* God is immutable. Jesus Christ remains the same (Heb. 13:8). He is God and changes not (Mal. 3:6). There is no variableness or shadow of turning with Him (James 1:17). Light is *active* and *irresistible*, and it shines in darkness. Darkness is incapable of overcoming it and is forced to retreat.

Light is *pure*. It is incapable of adulteration and suffers no admixture. The Lord Jesus Christ, the Light of the world, walked among the sons of men. He came into contact with all kinds of evil and filth. He talked with an adulterous woman and cleansed her of her sins. He also cleansed the leper. Nevertheless, as the sun shines on a dunghill without contamination, so Jesus Christ remained impeccable.

2. God's *light shines into the hearts of His elect to regenerate them.* Light is irresistible. The Holy Spirit causes the light of God to illuminate His own. In God's light, they see light (Ps. 36:9). "For God, who commanded the light to shine out of darkness, hath shined in our hearts, to give the light of the knowledge of the glory of God in the face of Jesus Christ" (II Cor. 4:6).

3. God's *light reveals sin in the lives of the regenerate.* The light that shone into their hearts to regenerate them continues to shine to reveal sin in their lives. Three faults of Christians, and the provisions for them, are explained in I John 1:6—2:2. Each begins with the phrase, "if we say" (1:6, 8, 10). (1) If a Christian says he has fellowship with the Lord but walks in darkness, he lies and does not the truth (v. 6). Cleansing for the first fault results from walking in the light (v. 7). (2) If a Christian says he has no sin, he deceives himself and the truth is not in him (v. 8). Cleansing for the second fault results from confession of sin (v. 9). (3) If a Christian says he has not sinned, he makes God a liar, and God's Word is not in him (v. 10). Cleansing for the third fault is the advocacy of Jesus Christ (2:1-2).

If a Christian says he fellowships with the Lord but walks in darkness, he lies and does not the truth (I John 1:6). Holiness and wisdom is light, but wickedness and folly is darkness. Truth is light, but error is darkness. Every privileged relationship carries corresponding responsibility. Wherever the Holy Spirit functions, one must deal with the problem of sin. One who claims to have fellowship with God, but walks in darkness, lies. Ignorance of truth excuses no one. Consequently, children of light who live contrary to truth walk in spiritual darkness.

Christians filled with earthly aspirations experience a diminishing interest in the Word of God. Their concern about spiritual things wanes, and they backslide. A person who talks about truth without walking therein indicates he is walking in darkness.

The corrective for walking in darkness is to be sanctified and cleansed by the blood of Jesus Christ (I John 1:7). He who knows truth and continually walks therein follows the path that grows brighter: "But the path of the just is as the shining light, that shineth more and more unto the perfect day" (Prov. 4:18).

If a Christian says he has no sin, he deceives himself and the truth is not in him (I John 1:8). The person claiming present sinlessness because of personal salvation deceives himself. He incorrectly reports his state. The old sin nature remains in every regenerate person. Unless a believer walks in the light, the old nature will be manifested. Christians with unconfessed sins flee, seeking shelter from Scriptural light.

Christians are cleansed from their sins when they confess them to God (I John 1:9). Restorative forgiveness is *conditional*. Unconfessed sin does not remove salvation, because everlasting forgiveness is *unconditional*. It does, however, require God's chastening.

Before anyone will break with sin, he must desire to be rid of it. "He that covereth his sins shall not prosper: but whoso confesseth and forsaketh them shall have mercy" (Prov. 28:13). When one accustoms himself to sinning he becomes unaware of it. The Book of Job was written to instruct Christians how to abhor sin in themselves and to repent. The proclamation of doctrine reaches the hearts of sinning Christians and causes them to repent.

At the root of almost every church problem is unconfessed, secret sin. Confession at the private altar is
sufficient to secure forgiveness and cleansing for sin
known only to God and an individual soul, but forgiveness of public sin necessitates confession to one another.
Worship is impossible for those who have sinned against
one another, until they have righted the wrong (Matt.
5:23-24).

Forgiveness is costly. God forgives a repentant sinner
because of the Savior's sacrifice. In the same way, it
costs the forgiving heart to forgive another's transgression. But it is worth the price, for forgiven ones have
forgiving spirits. Flesh does not easily yield, but Christians are not debtors to the flesh—they crucify the flesh
(I Cor. 9:27).

With one exception sins committed *before* a person
was saved should never be related. They were washed
away in the blood of the Lord Jesus Christ. To continue
to publicly confess sins committed before justification is
insulting and injurious to the finished work of Jesus
Christ. He everlastingly forgave the sinner of them. To
reiterate those sins calls attention to oneself. Present-
day evangelism capitalizes on repeated confessions from
former dope addicts, prize fighters, convicts, and so on.
Dragging hearers through the mire is not necessary to
regenerate and convert those who hear. The experiences
of others regenerate no one. God alone regenerates.

There is only *one* circumstance where sins committed
before justification should be confessed. A saved person
will follow Zacchaeus's example of *making amends* to
those he wronged before his conversion (Luke 19:1-10).
Zacchaeus made reparation to persons he had wronged
during his unsaved condition. The apostle Paul related
sins he committed before his conversion for the same
reason. The historical account was given by Luke
(Acts 9). Paul repeated it to the Hebrews (Acts 22), to
the Gentiles (Acts 26), in relation to God's sovereignty
(Gal. 1:13-17), to show its separateness from all human

merit (Phil. 3), and as a pattern to Timothy (I Tim. 1:12-17).

If a Christian says he has not sinned, he makes God a liar, and God's Word is not in him (I John 1:10). Sin is present in every believer and in order to retain fellowship with God it must be confessed. Correction for sinning is a part of Christ's advocacy (I John 2:1-2).

Christians are children of light: "For ye were sometimes darkness, but now are ye light in the Lord . . ." (Eph. 5:8). As such, Christians must reflect God's light "and have no fellowship with the unfruitful works of darkness, but rather reprove them" (Eph. 5:11). The ministry of light does not terminate in believers. Light was wrought in them by the Holy Spirit that His mission in the world should be accomplished through them. They work out the salvation God wrought within (Phil. 2:12-13); God works in them to will and to do His good pleasure.

Light reflects its *source*. Every sunbeam calls attention to the mighty source of energy from which it springs. A Christian who reflects God's light calls attention not to himself but to God. When his light shines before men, he glorifies the Father who is in heaven (Matt. 5:16).

Transformers break down electrical voltage, making it safe for human use. The light of God could not be looked upon until it was "stepped down." No one has ever beheld God's essential glory. He veiled His glory— "stepped down" His light—when Jesus Christ became flesh. Then, men beheld His moral glory: "And the Word was made flesh, and dwelt among us, (and we beheld his glory, the glory as of the only begotten of the Father,) full of grace and truth" (John 1:14). That light is made to shine through recipients of God's grace.

By its very nature, light opposes darkness. Light and darkness cannot make a truce. One who continually pursues darkness without reproving it is naturally dark. But Christians are not in darkness, although they may temporarily walk in darkness when they walk contrary to truth. This will cause a loss of fellowship, but this fellowship may be restored by walking in the light, confessing sins, and relying on the advocacy of the Lord Jesus Christ.

7

Confession Included in Restorative Forgiveness

God is the author of forgiveness—He alone can forgive sin. Sinners have profaned His name, abused His patience, violated His laws, and stained His glory. Nevertheless, He forgives them of their sin. Because of everlasting forgiveness, sins committed by believers are hidden from the eyes of the Father. The blood of Jesus Christ covers all sin—past, present, and future.

Although a believer's sins are hidden from the Father, they must be duly confessed and cleansed. The justified person retains his sin nature; therefore, he requires continual sanctification.

Sinning Christians lose the *joy* of their salvation. Everlastingly forgiven persons alone experience joy. (Joy cannot be *restored* to those who have never experienced it.) The restoration of one who through sin had lost the joy of his salvation is recorded in Psalms 32 and 51. Jacob also was restored to the fellowship he had previously enjoyed at Bethel (Gen. 31:3; 32:9; 35:1-15). The Ephesian saints who had left their first love were exhorted to return (Rev. 2:1-5).

The introduction to Psalm 32, as recorded in verses 1 and 2, describes the joy experienced by a forgiven sinner. David recognized the radical nature of sin (v. 3-7), and the Lord answered his confession of sin (vs.

8-9). The psalm concludes (vs. 10-11) with a testimony to God's redeeming grace.

The psalm is introduced with an expression of overflowing joy because of forgiven sins. The writer rejoiced over forgiven *acts* of sin. In Psalm 51 he rejoiced over the forgiven *nature* of sin. Erroneous concepts of forgiveness result from ignorance of that distinction.

The Lord pronounced David blessed because he had been everlastingly forgiven. That forgiveness was based on the everlasting covenant that God the Father had made with His Son and on Christ's finished work on the cross. Regenerated persons are blessed because they are in a better state than Adam was before he fell. Christians do not bemoan Adam's fall, but rejoice that they are trophies of God's grace. Future blessings are also promised (Rev. 21—22).

One whose *transgression* is forgiven is blessed. This one word does not adequately convey the meaning here. It is called "transgression," "sin," and "iniquity" (Ps. 32:1, 2, 5). *Transgression* is rebellion against rightful authority. *Sin* is missing the mark. *Iniquity* is moral crookedness. Three expressions for pardon are also given: "forgiven," "covered," and "not imputed" (vs. 1-2). *Forgiven* signifies taken away. *Covered* indicates that sins are hidden from God's face. *Nonimputation* means the debt has been canceled; it is not reckoned to the sinner's account.

Believers are blessed with *assurance* that the sins they commit after their regeneration will not be imputed to their accounts. Repentance and confession of sin are *fruits* of Christ's advocacy. The Lord Jesus Christ righteously settled the sin question on the cross: consequently, He righteously pleads for believers on the throne. Past, present, and future sins of believers were judged in the sacrifice of the Lord Jesus Christ.

Believers *without guile* (hyprocrisy) are blessed. Sincerity and hypocrisy are incompatible. Guile is manifested by refusing to seriously consider oneself before

God. Such persons inevitably excuse themselves for not confessing their sin. Frivolous amusement and religious ceremonies are often adopted in order to relieve the labor of reflection. A forgiven person, on the other hand, openly confesses his sin and makes no excuse for it. He desires impartial treatment. He studies God's Word and implements what he has learned by following practical holiness.

David recognized the radical nature of sin, felt the burden and sorrow thereof, and confessed it. He recognized that all sin is against the Lord. He looked retrospectively from his restored fellowship to his forgiven backsliding (Ps. 32:3-4). During his silence—failure to confess his sins—he suffered God's chastening. Failure to confess sin may result from thoughtlessness, pride, or procrastination. Sin is never diminished by deferred confession. It not only is wrong, it is not worthwhile.

David's state after his great transgression is reflected in Psalm 51. His decline was marked by various complications which not only aggravated his personal guilt but directly affected the lives of others.

A Christian's sin is the most heinous of all iniquities. An unsaved person may be guilty of all kinds of sin, but it is a Christian's sin that brings reproach upon the One who has everlastingly forgiven him.

David's sin resulted in the loss of four things: (1) He lost his *peace* and prayed for *forgiveness* (v. 1). His pleading for forgiveness began with requesting mercy before mentioning his sin. He did not plead past purity, pious parentage, public position, or accomplishments for the Lord. (2) He lost his *purity* and prayed for *cleansing* (v. 2). His plea was for personal cleansing—wash *me*—not for cleansing of his garments. Hypocrites are satisfied with garment cleansing. Sincere Christians desire internal cleansing. (3) He lost the *joy of his salvation* and pleaded for *restoration* (vs. 4-12). Many become sick from sin, but David was sick *of* sin *as sin*. He made full confession. None but truly born-again persons will fully confess before the all-seeing eye of God. (4) He lost his *power*—effectiveness in service—and prayed for its *renewal* (vs. 13-19).

Five grand themes dominate Psalm 51: (1) *Sin*—Sin is regarded in three ways. It is a blotted record that must be wiped out. It is a polluted robe that must be washed. It is a deadly disease from which one must be cleansed. (2) *Responsibility*—David did not blame heredity, environment, society, instinct, or circumstances for his sin. He acknowledged his own guilt. Those who seek to excuse sin know nothing of the grace of God. (3) *Repentance*—Old Testament saints could understand from prophecy that a fountain is opened for cleansing (Zech. 13:1). All the saved since the death of the Testator know there is a fountain filled with blood drawn from Immanuel's veins that cleanses from all sin (I John 1:7). (4) *Forgiveness*—Consciousness of sin leads the believer to that fountain filled with blood. (5) *Testimony*—Forgiveness and cleansing lead to a life of witnessing for the Lord. A redeemed person cannot refrain from daily witnessing.

Before he confessed his sins David's bones waxed old (Ps. 32:3). His physical strength diminished. The sapping of a person's spiritual state affects his physical well-being. A person suffering from foreign matter in his eye may not enjoy his eyesight any more than one who is blind. Nevertheless, no one would conclude that he had lost his eyesight. Removal of the disturbing foreign matter is often painful. Similarly, removal of that which is foreign to spirituality is painful to the offending Christian.

God's chastening hand was heavy upon David (v. 4). Scientists affirm that the atmosphere weighs on all solid objects a certain amount of pressure per square inch. However, they are not crushed. Likewise, a Christian is is protected *through* God's chastening (Ps. 89:3-34).

David repented and confessed his sin (Ps. 32:5-7). His confession was threefold: (1) He *acknowledged* his sin.

(2) He *uncovered* his sin. (3) He *confessed* his sin. The psalmist's grateful testimony after his restoration is recorded in Psalm 32:6-7. The Lord answered David's confession with instruction (v. 8) and warning (v. 9).

Christians cannot be instructed and blessed until they acknowledge, uncover, and confess their sins. Instruction *follows* genuine confession of sin. Truth must be learned through this kind of practical experience. The ability to quote portions of Scripture is insufficient. Abstract truth alone—truth separated from practical consideration or application—profits no one. God's people must be indoctrinated. Persons may be theoretically indoctrinated and give mental and vocal assent to doctrine. However, only when doctrine is received into a believer's heart can he exhibit its molding influence.

Confession, forgiveness, and restoration to fellowship with the Lord enable Christians to effectually serve the Lord. When David was restored to the joy of his salvation, he was then in a position to faithfully witness for the Lord (Ps. 51:12-13). The thirteenth verse expresses a result, *"Then* will I teach transgressors thy ways . . ." and a resolve, ". . . and sinners shall be converted unto thee." When a penitent is cleansed and filled with joy, he must speak. When he is endued with power, he must achieve.

A true penitent recognizes that sin is against God, and that the root of sin is his own corrupt nature. Sin requires a remedy, for sin deprives a believer of the joy of his salvation and robs him of his power to witness for the Lord.

8

Fruitfulness Produced Through Restorative Forgiveness

_____ HOSEA 14:1-9 _____

Revived believers have spiritual beauty and strength of character. They become fruitful and they grow as the vine because they discipline their lives. The Lord enables them to produce fruit, for all fruit is from the Lord (I Cor. 15:10). No person produces fruit apart from Him.

The Book of Hosea was written to correct Israel's backsliding, and a message for God's people of all time is contained therein. Christians do not suddenly fall. Backsliders begin to slide slowly—effortlessly, naturally. It may even be a pleasant sensation. When the pace begins to accelerate, however, joy will give way to alarm.

Hosea was the prophet in Israel's zero hour, and his message was to sinning believers. Hosea understood the true meaning of Israel's sin—it was spiritual adultery and whoredom. Those who seek satisfaction through unlawful practices or relations are guilty of spiritual adultery or whoredom. Christians are warned against such sin: "Ye adulterers and adulteresses, know ye not that the friendship of the world is enmity with God? whosoever therefore will be a friend of the world is the enemy of God" (James 4:4). Things of the world are passing away

(I Cor. 7:31). Christians who court the world are guilty of spiritual adultery.

No transgression is so heinous as that of those who are disloyal to known truth. They sin against *light* and *love*. Forgiveness must not be viewed in the light of only one of God's attributes—love. Three of His attributes are predominant in Hosea's prophecy: (1) God is *holy;* therefore, Israel's sin was intolerable (chaps. 1—7). God's holiness, not His love, is first in order. It is when one views his sin in the light of God's holiness that he can see its seriousness. (2) God is *just*; therefore, Israel was punished (chaps. 8—10). (3) God is *love*; therefore, Israel was restored (chaps. 11—14). Christians are comforted with the knowledge that God forgives His own in love.

The first three verses of Hosea 14 introduce the chapter. Throughout the Old Testament the words *turn* or *return* signify repentance. Hosea exhorted Israel to repent. The necessity for repentance indicates that one has sinned. That is *humbling.* God made provision for the sins of all of His own. That is *encouraging.* Conclusively, the word *return* both encourages and humbles Christians.

The following important concepts appear in the introduction to Hosea 14: (1) An awful fact is stated—*thou hast fallen.* The children of Israel had fallen by their own iniquity; they were believers, but they had backslidden from a higher to a lower state. Christians do not remain on a single plateau. They are either progressing or regressing. Their desire should be continual progress. Regression in Christians is always grievous. Their fall is not attributable to circumstances; although their circumstances may reveal their inward desires which cause them to lust. (2) Israel was affectionately *exhorted to return* to the Lord. (3) They were given *instructive direction.* Our opportunity dictates the degree of our responsibility. Israel was admonished to be sincere in confession and prayer. "The calves of our lips" has reference to the sacrifice of lips, and that includes truthfulness and praise. (4) Israel was *warned* against placing confidence in the creature (v. 3). Neither circumstances nor individuals can deliver anyone. When God alters one's heart to repentance, He alone removes carnal confidence. Repentant persons recognize God's all-sufficiency to satisfy their desires. They find their mercy and satisfaction in Him.

Three primary thoughts appear in Hosea 14:4-9—(1) God restores backsliders (v. 4). (2) The dew of heaven symbolizes the method God uses to restore backsliders (v. 5). (3) God's restoration of backsliders is effective (vs. 6-9).

1. *God restores backsliding believers:* "I will heal . . . I will love . . . I will be . . ." (vs. 4-5). A backslidden person and an apostate person differ in that there is no hope for apostates. They have heard the truth and have come to some knowledge of it. They profess Christianity but turn from their knowledge of truth. Born-again persons may backslide, but their backsliding is not fatal. God's people are strongly inclined to backslide, but the Lord loves them freely. That love is not incited by man—it is impelled by God alone. God grants repentance; He alone enables a sinning believer to repent.

2. Dew symbolizes *God's method of restoration.* "I will be as the dew" (v. 5). Dew comes silently when the winds are hushed and the night is still. It has a reviving effect on vegetation. It represents the Holy Spirit's work of restoring believers: "Not by might, nor by power, but by my spirit, saith the Lord of hosts" (Zech. 4:6). (*Dew* in Hosea 6:4 is contrasted with *dew* in chapter 14:5. The first shows that man's goodness soon passes. Contrarily, the second shows that restoration by the Holy Spirit refreshes.)

Dew symbolizes the Spirit's restoration of sinning believers. It is heaven-born and it descends silently. The Holy Spirit works silently in the hearts of His people, giving them strength and conviction to do the will of God. The nature of dew is to soften and moisten. Only the Holy Spirit can soften calloused hearts. He causes confession, restoration, cleanliness, and the bearing of fruit. Dew falls after the sun has withdrawn its shining. The Lord Jesus told His disciples that it was expedient that He go away. It was after He ascended to the Father, withdrawing His personal presence from the earth, that the Holy Spirit came. Dew is supplied daily, and the Holy Spirit gives daily strength to meet a Christian's need. The joy of restoration recalls first deliverance. The soul is brought to a fresh starting point and becomes a fragrant garden.

3. *God's restoration of backsliders is effective* (vs. 5-6). They grow as a lily. Lilies often grow in unseemly places where their beauty is outstanding. They sometimes spring up in the midst of storm. In the same way, restored believers radiate the beauty of Christianity. Dew causes lilies to grow; and the Holy Spirit produces spiritual growth in restored believers.

But beauty alone is insufficient; restored backsliders need strength. God promises restored believers the strength of Lebanon. The cedar of Lebanon with its roots and spreading branches is symbolic of this kind of strength. One who has been restored to fellowship not only manifests beauty; he also has spiritual strength of character. The branches of the restored one spread as the fruitful branches of an olive tree. The aroma of those who have been restored is as Lebanon, denoting the fragrance of a fruitful life. Restored ones grow as a vine (this also signifies the necessity for pruning).

God restoratively forgives sinners because the Lord Jesus Christ is their Advocate. He reveals that His character is Light by His restorative forgiveness. Individual Christians must confess their sins to God to receive His forgiveness. Not until then can they bring forth fruit to glorify the Lord.

9

God's Governmental
Forgiveness

_____ DANIEL 1:1-21 _____

Governmental forgiveness is based on unchangeable divine principles. Every child of God should seriously consider the subject of governmental forgiveness. A sin is not necessarily done with even when it is confessed and the confessor is forgiven. One who has been everlastingly forgiven may sin and be restoratively forgiven, yet every Christian must reap in this life what he sows (Gal. 6:7).

While God delays exercising His power (Ps. 50:21), He does chasten His children who have been restored from backsliding. No time can be as solemn as the living present. Divine principles must be maintained because they are unchangeable. Christians, whether young or old, should maintain the high principles of God's Word. Like Daniel, regardless of the social, monetary, or personal cost, they should not lower them.

Israel's history proves that God judges Christians in this life for the sins they commit. Several judgments are mentioned in connection with Israel's history: (1) servitude, (2) captivity, and (3) desolations. Because of the national sins of Israel, Judah was brought under seventy years of servitude to Babylon (Dan. 1:1). Israel continued to rebel under servitude; therefore, God sent them more severe punishment. He brought them into captivity. Israel remained rebellious in captivity, and the Lord sent desolations upon them.

Daniel's prophecy reveals God's governmental forgiveness of Israel while they were in Babylonian captivity. It is significant that the name *Daniel* comes from two Hebrew words: *Dan*, which means to judge, and *el*, which refers to God. Hence, his name means, "God judging." There are six basic divisions in Daniel's prophecy: (1) Heathen *customs* are judged (chap. 1); (2) heathen *philosophy* is judged (chap. 2); (3) heathen *pride* is judged (chaps. 3—4); (4) heathen *impiety* is judged (chap. 5); (5) heathen *persecutors* are judged (chap. 6); (6) heathen *nations* are judged (chaps. 7—12).

The four captured young men (1:6) were "children in whom was no blemish, but well favoured, and skilful in all wisdom, and cunning in knowledge, and understanding science . . ." (1:4). The king, desiring to benefit from everything, saw great potential in those young men.

The devout young men were offered a three-year course in the school of the heathen at the king's expense (1:5). The Babylonians sought to persuade them to surrender their convictions and principles. The world today uses the same tactics, still seeking to persuade Christians to relinquish their convictions and principles.

The names of the four young men were changed at the request of the king (1:7; 5:12). He hoped that changing their names would convince them to forget their allegiance to God. (Their Hebrew names signified that Daniel and his companions were associated with Jehovah God.) The prince of the eunuchs, at the king's command, changed their names, but he could not change their characters.

Although the Hebrew children were subjected to the dictates of the heathen king, they remained committed to divine principles. Divinely appointed persons will refuse any appointment by men who ignore God's appointment. Biblical principles have little influence on one who is not committed to them. To a Christian truly following the Lord, however, the customs around him may change, but his commitment to biblical principles cannot.

Daniel refused to defile himself (Dan. 1:8), and he was willing to be tested (v. 12). The prince of the eunuchs feared that the physical condition of the Hebrew youths would deteriorate because of their decision not to eat the king's appointed menu. Unsaved people know nothing of the sustenance of God. Children of God have a meat to eat that the world knows nothing about. Daniel chose a simple life. The less complicated a Christian's life is, the easier it is to live close to the Lord. Too often well-intentioned men today, caught up in a religious society, advocate complicated programs instead of living simple lives with the goal of honoring the Lord.

Daniel did not falter under temptation. He could not prevent his name change, but he purposed in his heart not to defile himself by compromise. Spiritual courage enabled Daniel to properly call the king's program *defilement.* That which is not of God does defile. Erroneous teaching defiles Christians; they must turn from it to that which honors the Lord.

It is generally agreed that Daniel was sixteen years of age when he was captured. His youth did not hinder his conviction and willingness to stand for the Lord. The same grace that enabled Daniel to remain true to divine principles enables saved children, young people, and adults to do the same today. God's grace in the life of a young person will enable him to live a godly life just as older persons, also recipients of grace, can.

God overruled and brought Daniel into favor with those in power. Although people may despise Christians for standing for divine principles, they must admit that those believers have something that they do not possess.

Daniel separated himself, and God gave him wisdom. His wisdom excelled the astrologers, soothsayers, and magicians. The humble, separated Christian can know more than the wisest men of the world. The way to gain knowledge is described in John 7:17—"If any man will do his will, he shall know of the doctrine, whether it be of God, or whether I speak of myself." It is a lack of obedience to the will of God that prevents a person from discerning whether a thing is of God or not. The more obedient a Christian is to what he knows, the more the Lord reveals to him.

10

Governmental Forgiveness Through Cursed Blessings

God's governmental forgiveness is also revealed in Malachi's prophecy. God warned Israel's spiritual leaders that He would curse their blessings (Mal. 2:1-9). The message was directed primarily to spiritual leaders, but it is applicable to all who know the Lord Jesus Christ. Malachi's prophecy has many points in common with Christ's warning to the Christians in Laodicea (Rev. 3:14-22). Malachi preached to a group of people who had been revived about one hundred years before under Haggai and Zechariah. That revival was short-lived, however, and Malachi faced conditions similar to those faced by the men of God today.

Malachi's rebuke of the priests begins in chapter 1, verse 6 and is completed in chapter 2, verse 9. The second chapter describes continuation of *blessing with curse upon it.* Insensibility to God's blessing was the great sin of the Israelites. Their guilt was compounded by their failure to recognize their sin. When they were confronted with Scripture, they sought to justify themselves. Their condition was much like the chaotic condition of professing Christendom today.

Malachi's dialogue style of writing was unique. Throughout his prophecy, he illustrated Israel's insensibility to God's love and goodness. (1) The Lord said, "I have loved you....." The Israelites replied, "Wherein hast thou loved us?" (1:2).(2) The Lord said, "O priests, that despise my name...." They replied, "Wherein have we despised thy name?" (1:6).(3) The Lord said, "Ye offer polluted bread upon mine altar...." The priests replied "Wherein have we polluted thee?" (1:7).(4) The Lord accused them of profaning His name. They were showing more concern for the creature than for the Creator. They replied that the table of the Lord was polluted and that worship was wearisome (1:12-13). (5) Judah profaned the holiness of the Lord by intermarriage. They asked, "Wherefore?" (2:11-16). (6) They wearied the Lord with their words. They asked, "Wherein have we wearied him?" (2:17). (7) They had gone away from the Lord's ordinances, and the Lord commanded them to return. They asked, "Wherein shall we return?" (3:7). (8) They were reminded that they had robbed God of tithes and offerings. They asked, "Wherein have we robbed thee?" (3:8). (9) They were told that their words were stout against the Lord. They asked, "What have we spoken so much against thee?" (3:13). (10) They were accused of saying it was vain to serve the Lord. They inquired how they might profit from serving Him (3:14).

The priests had become like the people to whom they ministered. That was forbidden by the Lord. Men of God should set an example for the people, for fervent teaching apart from fervent living accomplishes nothing.

Malachi's burden (1:1) was not self-imposed. It was laid upon him by the Lord. God's message is called a burden to the man of God. (1) It condemns sin, exposes hypocrisy, and causes division wherever it is truthfully proclaimed. (2) Every man to whom it is committed must give an account of the way he has treated that message when he stands before God. True preaching is artesian; it wells up from within. Men to whom God has given the burden of His message cannot hold it within. They cannot but speak the things they have seen and heard (Acts. 4:20). They cry with Paul, "Woe is unto me, if I preach not the gospel!" (I Cor. 9:16).

Nothing disturbs true children of God more than those who question the authenticity of God's Word. Malachi faced that problem in Israel's unawareness to God's blessing and their own sin. They questioned everything pertaining to God and themselves. However, God met every criticism they presented.

Man's first instinct is to rebel against divine sovereignty. But there was a faithful remnant during Malachi's time, as there was in the church at Laodicea. The true spiritual remnant shall look upon the overthrow of the wicked, not to delight in their ruin but because it declares God's glory and testifies to the integrity of His spiritual remnant (Mal. 1:5). The lesson that may be learned here by the church of the Lord Jesus Christ is recorded in II Thessalonians 1:3-8.

Three things should be observed about Malachi 1:5: (1) It is a prophetical utterance; (2) the prophecy shall be fulfilled at Christ's second advent: ". . . your eyes shall see, and ye shall say . . ."; (3) " . . . the Lord will be magnified from the border of Israel."

Israel was insensitive to God's love and to her own sin (Mal. 1:2). Ignorance about oneself is ignorance of the worst kind. Israel did not reverence and honor God's name (Mal. 1:6). They did not fear Him. Today, God's name, His day (the Lord's day), His word (the Holy Scripture), His ordinances, and His ministers are dishonored. Nothing should prevent Christians from assembling to worship on the Lord's day and hearing the Word of God as God's message to their individual hearts. Every Christian should follow the Lord in baptism, become a member of a New Testament church, and observe the Lord's Supper. They should highly esteem God's ministers for their work's sake (I Thess. 5:12-13).

The people of Israel manifested their sin and irreverence for God by the offerings they made to Him (Mal. 1:7-8). They offered to God what they would not offer to the governor. The law demanded that they should honor God with their best. Leftover time, money, energy, and talents are unacceptable to God. If Christians fail to offer their best, God will curse their blessings.

The Israelites refused to perform any act of worship without remuneration (Mal. 1:10). Christians should assemble at the Lord's house to receive guidance and to worship the Lord in spirit and truth. They should desire spiritual, not monetary, blessings.

Incorrect worship is worse than no worship at all. People often say, "Well, I'm glad so-and-so is going to church *some* place; he is giving some semblance of religion." However, unless he worships in spirit and truth, he desecrates the name of God. Pure offerings must come from a *purified* heart, a *penitent* and *obedient* spirit and a spirit that is *consecrated* to God (Mal. 1:10-14).

Malachi described continued blessing with a curse upon it (Mal. 2). How does God curse a person's blessing? (1) He may make one poor in his wealth. The Laodiceans boasted of their wealth, thinking they had need of nothing. The Lord pronounced them poor. This affluent age is experiencing wealth such as has never before been known. Nevertheless, spirituality is at a very low ebb. (2) He may make one sick in his health—a person may boast of physical health and become so occupied with it that he becomes spiritually ill. (3) He may cause one to become ignorant in his knowledge. God may curse a person's worldly knowledge so that he will be made spiritually ignorant. Knowledge and wisdom of the world superabound today. Men are "ever learning, and never able to come to the knowledge of the truth" (II Tim. 3:7). Thus, knowledge is cursed so that it becomes ignorance. (4) He may make one a failure in his success. Absorption in one's accomplishments becomes a curse if God deprives him of the power to enjoy them.

Malachi's message was directed primarily to the priests—the spiritual leaders of his day. God's message of rebuke continues to direct itself to spiritual leaders, those who represent the Lord. The Lord expressed His dissatisfaction with the priests of Malachi's time, saying, "... I will curse your blessings: yea, I have cursed them already, because ye do not lay it to heart. Behold, I will corrupt your seed, and spread dung upon your faces, even the dung of your solemn feasts; and one shall take you away with it" (Mal. 2:2-3).

Under the Levitical system, carcasses of sacrificed animals, with their refuse, were burned outside the camp. A cart carried them to that designated place. The Lord warned the sinning priests that He would spread on their faces the refuse from the animals offered in pretense of worship. Furthermore, He would allow them to be taken away on those despicable carts to the place of shame.

Ministers of the Lord are responsible not to sin against the Lord. They must render their best to Him. Those who devote much time to social organizations and activities have nothing spiritual to give the people. They, like the priests of Malachi's day, may be removed with the refuse to a place of shame.

11

Reaping What Is Sown Through Governmental Forgiveness

—————— II SAMUEL 12:1-20 ——————

Believers reap in this life what they sow (Gal. 6:7-9). Although they confess their sins, they must experience governmental forgiveness. God's men who are not practically holy bring reproach on Jesus Christ. They give occasion for the enemies of the Lord to blaspheme. King David, a child of God, grievously sinned against the Lord. He confessed his sin, and the Lord put it away (II Sam. 12:13). In spite of the fact that he confessed, was forgiven, and was promised that he would not suffer death because of his sin, David caused the enemies of the Lord to blaspheme (II Sam. 12:14). Consequently, he experienced governmental forgiveness. The sword never departed from his house (II Sam. 12:10).

David's fall had serious consequences but it was not fatal. He fell, but he was not utterly cast down (Ps. 37:24). Christians may fall, but they do not become apostate. Notice the steps that preceded David's downfall which occurred after the end of the year (II Sam. 11:1). (At the end of one's days it is just as important to redeem the time, because the days are evil. Christians should continually take inventory of their lives.)

The events preceding David's fall are recorded in II Samuel 2: (1) He failed to endure the difficult life of

75

a soldier. (2) He indulged in a life of ease. (3) He allowed his eye to wander.

David took seven steps in his sinful indulgence: (1) He committed the crime of *adultery* (II Sam. 11:1-5). That included, as it always does, the sin of robbery and murder of character. Under the Jewish law, that was a capital offense. It remains thus. King David and his subject, Uriah, were on the same level so far as the law of God is concerned. The same law that governs every citizen of a country governs its rulers. (2) David attempted *deception* to prevent his crime from becoming known (vs. 6-11). (3) David made Uriah *drunk* (v. 13). (4) David manifested *ingratitude* and *injustice* toward Uriah by plotting his death. (5) David manifested *meanness* and *treachery* against Uriah. (6) David *involved another* (Joab) in his unjust act to clear his own crime. (7) David had Uriah *murdered.*

David's sin proves that no one sin stands alone. A man is tempted when he is drawn away by his own lust and enticed. Then, his lust conceives and brings forth sin (James 1:14-15). The little pitted speck rots inwardly, slowly spoiling the fruit of useful character. The little foxes spoil the vines (Song of Sol. 2:15). One sin is followed by a greater unless it is recognized and confessed.

The consequences of David's transgression are recorded in II Samuel 12. To awaken David to a sense of his wickedness, the Lord sent neither enemies to lay his country waste nor terrors to take hold on him. Instead, He sent one of His most faithful servants, Nathan.

God's message to David did not cause him to become enraged at Nathan. The king became indignant toward the guilty man portrayed in Nathan's parable. (A person can be indignant at another's failures but amazingly tender toward his own!) Nathan used David's own tongue as a lance to rip—and heal—his heart. David was horrified when he was convicted by Nathan's parable and confessed, "I have sinned against the Lord" (II Sam. 12:13). Unlike Adam, he did not shift the blame.

When a Christian's sins of disobedience, neglect, complacency, and so forth are pointed out by God's messenger, he should not become angry at the messenger or try to shift the blame. Instead, he should follow David's example of confession.

The principle of evil that resided in David exists in every born-again person. He is bent on backsliding (Hos. 11:7). No one harbors impurities in his thoughts without revealing them in his life. Although David's deceit was portentous, real honesty (which was the fruit of God's grace) remained in him during that self-deceiving time.

David revealed hatred for the person Nathan described; then Nathan said, "*Thou* art the man" (II Sam. 12:7). Although David confessed his sin and was forgiven, he experienced governmental forgiveness. The remainder of his life was filled with perpetual sorrow. Many professing believers do as they please and then rush to the Lord, begging forgiveness. They may ignore the truth that they must suffer the consequences of their sin, but they shall reap what they have sown.

Since believers reap in this life what they sow, they are taught to guard against backsliding. They should watch for temptations and withstand them. They are also taught to be charitable toward fallen fellow believers, although not at the expense of justice. Moreover, they must be careful not to employ David's fall as an excuse for sin, presuming they will receive a similar restoration. To acknowledge David's sin is one thing; to excuse it is another. The Lord reveals the sins of His people not so we can imitate them but to warn us.

Instances in Jacob's life also emphasize governmental forgiveness. Jacob deceived his father Isaac (Gen. 27). Later, he was deceived by his uncle (Gen. 29) and by his own sons (Gen. 37). Jacob cheated his brother and was cheated by his uncle. Jacob was everlastingly forgiven and restoratively forgiven; he was also governmentally forgiven.

Perhaps the bitterest result of all fleshly sowing is that which the sinner reaps in his own family. Nathan's parable was literally fulfilled in David's life. David suffered severe governmental forgiveness. He had taken Uriah's wife to be his own wife. Nathan accused him of taking a poor man's only lamb (II Sam. 12:4). David pronounced his own judgment when he said that the guilty man must "restore the lamb fourfold, because he did this thing, and because he had no pity" (II Sam. 12:6).

As Nathan predicted, the sword never departed from David's family (II Sam. 12:10). Bathsheba's son died (II Sam. 12:15, 18)—the Lord took one lamb. David saw his own sin reproduced in his two sons: incest in Amnon and murder in Absalom (II Sam. 13)—Amnon, the second lamb, was slain (II Sam. 13:32). David's third son, Absalom—the third lamb—was slain by Joab's dagger (II Sam. 18:14). Adonijah—the fourth lamb—fell at the command of Solomon, David's son (I Kings 2:24-25). So David reaped fourfold in his own family what he had sown. The sword never departed from his house. Thus he was governmentally forgiven.

Governmental forgiveness will come upon everlastingly and restoratively forgiven Christians who refuse to take advantage of opportunities to grow in the grace and knowledge of the Lord. Negligence may be confessed and forgiven, but one cannot live his life over and get what he missed during his negligence.

An individual may become so occupied with his livelihood that he neglects his spiritual or physical health. He may ask God's forgiveness, but forgiveness gives no one assurance that his physical health shall be restored. God may curse his blessings so that he becomes poor in wealth, sick in health, or a failure in success. Christians must place preeminence on spiritual things. They cannot expect to reap a harvest of usefulness and fruitfulness if they neglect the Lord. Redeeming the time is of utmost importance (Eph. 5:16). Days that are past cannot be redeemed. One must take advantage of present opportunities.

Divine principles originate with God; therefore, they are unchangeable. Children of God must conform to those principles. Failure to do so will bring the chastening hand of God upon the disobedient—He will curse their blessings. Thus, they shall reap in this life what they sow: God everlastingly forgives a person when He regenerates him. He restoratively forgives the everlastingly forgiven one when he sins. In this life, He governmentally forgives the everlastingly and restoratively forgiven person.